Solos

Getting in Touch With the Real You

By

Carolyn Harvill

ISBN: 1-4107-0972-8 (e-book)
ISBN: 1-4107-0973-6 (Paperback)

This book is printed on acid free paper.

Illustration by Kim Hetherington
Book Cover by Carry Handley

1st Books - rev. 02/21/03

Acknowledgements

For those who have shared portions of my journey, their strengths and encouragements have been a sustaining power in my life.

Special thanks to my *Spiritual Director*, Lucie Lichtenstein. She has always been a true friend.

My family, Mom, Jim, and Tracy, have taught me many things, not the least of which is how to love.

Bob, thank you for always being ready to share with me your love and acceptance.

To Jesus, whose teachings told me for the first time that God loved me. Who over the years has shown me that the old song is true: "What a Friend I have in Jesus."

To my Dad for teaching me to reach out and live my dreams.

And for the authors whose works have been just what I needed, when I needed them.

Thank you,

Carolyn

This book is about *Solos*. Honoring whom we are, our full potential, our gifts and talents that make us unique.

The tools we use to discover these treasures are *Solos*. A *Solo* is a gift we give ourselves that will reveal to us who we are and equip us to be all we are meant to be.

Solos - Time we set aside from the distractions that fill our lives to be with and show respect for the only person who will share our entire lives - our self.

Solos
Contents

There is only one person who will be with you throughout your entire life. It is not your Mom, Dad, spouse, child, or dear friend from the first grade. That person is you. You will be there when you feel great disappointment, fear, hope, pain, love and joy. You will be there when you make decisions that make you proud and when you make decisions you wish you could change.

How much time have you invested in getting to know this most important person?

Great relationships are based on shared experiences and time listening to each other. Are you listening to <u>you</u>? Are you hearing the cries of <u>your</u> heart?

Spirituality is feeling and knowing you are connected to something greater than yourself. There are many ways of experiencing this connection; religious practices, meditation, teachers, firewalking...etc.

Connecting with yourself can be a clear and accessible path to greater awareness of your place in the universe and your oneness with the whole. This connection includes a sense of belonging.

This connection is the essence of Getting to know the real you! – Enabling you to live life more fully.

Know thyself

There is a world within you no one has ever seen;

A voice no one has ever heard ...

Not even you.

As yet unknown...you are your own seer

Your own interpreter.

And so with eyes and ears grown sharp for voice or sign

Listen well...not to these words

But to that inward voice...

That impulse beating in your heart like a far wave,

Turn to that source and you will find what no one has ever found...

A ground within you no one has ever seen...

A world beyond limits of your dream's horizon.

Paul Murray, Irish Poet

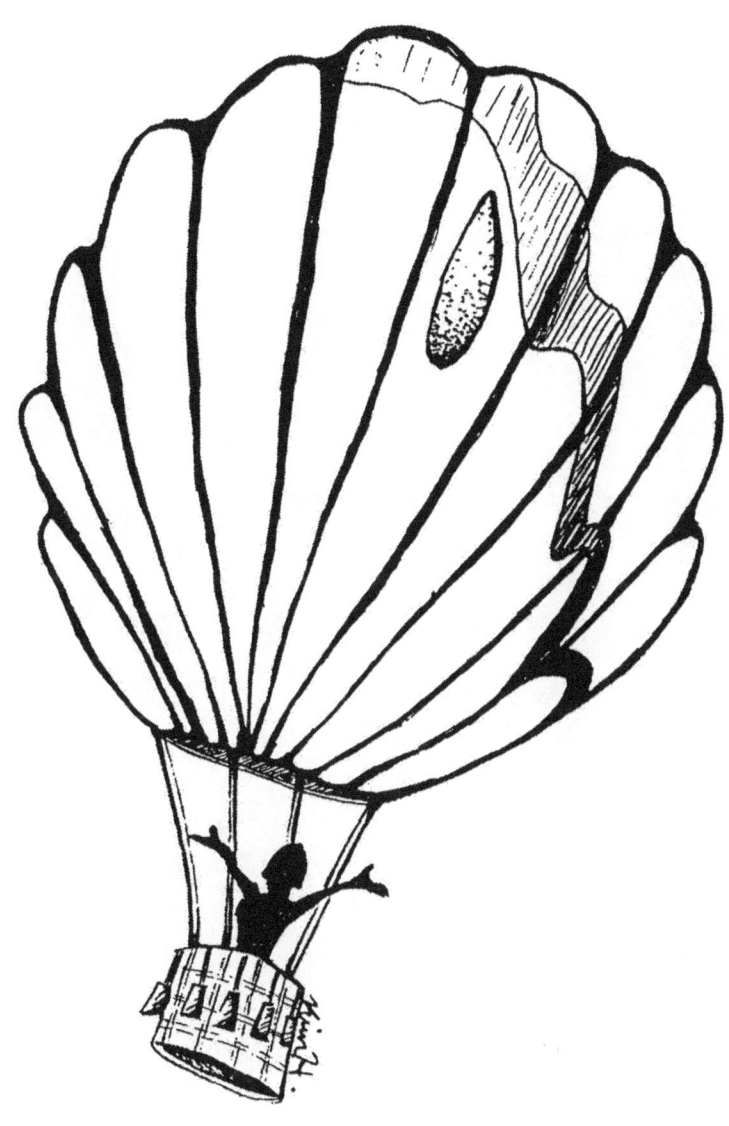

XV

Introduction

Have you ever been so looooww, a snake would need a ladder to scratch your belly? All of us have. When we take the time to get in touch with our inner core of uniqueness, we spend less time entertaining snakes who like ladders.

This book is about exploring our uniqueness through the use of solos. It's about spending more time at deeper levels of inspiration, peace, joy, sense of purpose and plain contentment with who we are. It stretches us to new heights and builds for us a solid foundation.

I was taking *Solos* long before I had a word to describe them.

I enjoyed creating moments for reflection and times to help me deal with what was happening around me. As you read this handbook, you too may say, "Oh, I know what she is talking about." Wonderful! This will be a tool for you to use to expand your experiences.

For others, this may open windows to whole new concepts.

This handbook is designed to meet you at your current stage and to encourage you to *Seek Out New Worlds*, those fascinating worlds residing within yourself. There you will find the strength, wisdom, creativity, and joy to create the life you desire.

If you have hesitated thinking that spirituality/connection/self-reflection is hard, or for more dedicated people, this book is for you. Reflecting on who we are and what our lives are about does not have to be hard. And, it is for everyone. Keep it simple. Keep it designed just for you and your lifestyle.

The first step is to try. To create these moments, you must lay aside the beliefs that there is only one way to succeed, that it is complicated, or that you can't do it. Dispel the idea that other people can, but you cannot. Everyone can. The first step is to say, "Yes, I will trust and honor myself by spending dedicated time with me."

Sure, let the experts help you. There is an abundance of resources. But, paraphrasing the words of that great Frank Sinatra song, *Do it your way*!

I have compiled this handbook to answer your basic questions and take the mystery and complexity out of creating these types of experiences. There is no one right way to get in touch with yourself and it doesn't have to be hard. The idea-list (found at the back of this book) will give you additional resources for enriching your experiences.

Trust yourself to create just the right experiences for you at any particular moment in time. And, if you find it hard to trust yourself, realize most of us started where you are. Put your trust in the desire that is calling and moving you toward knowing yourself. This awareness of a need is your call to wholeness. It will guide you and put in your path what you need; a book, a comment by a friend, a song, a beautiful flower, a feeling, or other important and inspiring signs. Your desire has a thousand voices that will speak to you in just the way you need to hear. Commit to listening.

CHAPTER 1

What does it mean to take a SOLO?

It means to create a time apart from the distractions of life to spend time with <u>you</u>. Taking a *Solo* is getting to know the <u>unique</u> you.

"There is a vitality, a life force, a quickening that is translated through you into action, and because there is only one of you in all time, this expression is unique. And if you block it, it will never exist through any medium and be lost. It is not your business to determine how good it is nor how it compares with other expressions. It is your business to keep it yours, clearly and directly."

Martha Graham

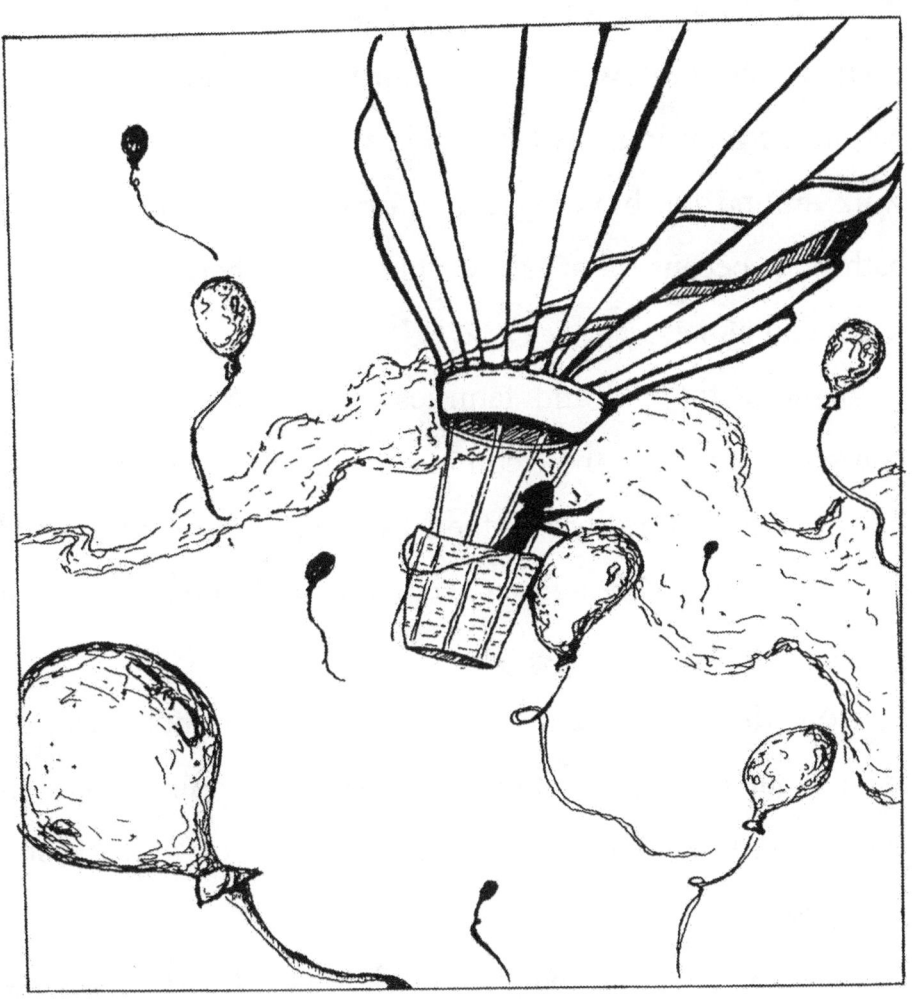

A *Solo* can be anything from a five-minute break to a month long vacation. It is when you set aside time for yourself; taking time apart from the distractions of life and from life itself, just for you to be with you.

It can be the few minutes before the children get out of bed in the morning, the ten minutes at lunch time when you walk around the building alone, or the five minutes in the bathroom because that is the only place where family will leave you alone.

Some with jobs and families, and seemingly too few hours in a day, use their commuting time in the car to turn off the radio and reflect on their lives. Our aim is not to add complexity, but simplicity. Our goal is to find moments that fit within our current lifestyle.

Don't be discouraged. Know that a few minutes can be carved out of any schedule. And at some point, you can expand your solo into a weekend re-treat or a weeklong vacation.

Some would say, " why should I add another thing to my 'to-do' list. The length of my list is what depresses me." This is the one thing on your to-do list that can help you prioritize the rest of your list and give you the courage and energy to accomplish those items at the top of your revised list.

Most of us start small with just a few minutes and then begin to build. A key is to give yourself permission to start slow and grow at your own pace. The one constant is that you do it alone. You don't share it with your children, your spouse, your mom, or even your best friend. You may choose to share parts of it with them later. Or, you may choose not to share it with another soul.

When you get to your multi-day *Solo,* (this may take years to accomplish), you will experience a freedom never before imagined. Do you want to sightsee? Great! Would you rather sit in the hot tub until you look like a prune? Wonderful. Will you read or will you sleep? Will you go to the beach or the mountains? The choice is yours. You write the directions with guidance from your heart.

Does that sound wonderful or scary? Maybe it feels like a combination of both. If you don't have a good time, you have no one to blame but yourself.

Some of us are not comfortable making decisions. It's easier to let others direct our lives. When you begin to make more decisions, it opens a world of new possibilities.

A question many ask - Is it really OK to please only myself? The truth? Yes it is!

Trust me on this point. When you get to the place that you trust yourself to be alone, you will have a wonderful time; a time of fun, reflection, and growth. Not always easy maybe, but it will be your own special time. You will learn about this person who is with you all of your life and strengthen your feeling and awareness of your spiritual connection to the *all* that is the universe around you.

Now, when you go on your *Solo* vacation and you get home and want to share all the fun with others, keep in mind what you have learned from other trips. There are people who will look at your pictures. Some will listen to some of your stories. Others will listen to as much and as often as you want to tell them. And, there are those who won't want to hear a thing, or see a single picture. Don't worry about it. Just treasure your memories and share with those who want to hear just as much as you want to share.

This is my first plug for a journal; it will not be my last. Even if you have never kept a journal before, buy a cheap notebook or a fancy leather bound journal and write down what you are doing, what you are seeing, what you are feeling and anything else that comes to mind. This will be a treasure of enjoyment for years to come. It is also a great tool for getting to know this special person in your life - you.

Sometimes we need to let go of past hurts or things that keep us stagnant. A journal can give us a place to express our emotions fully and then move on.

In our *Solos* we learn to know and accept who we are. With acceptance comes the power to change. All of our energy is no longer going into denying who we are or in our current situations, but into accepting who we are, and realizing that the ability to change is available to us.

A visual image – picture a small boat, on the Atlantic, in a storm of activity. That's you in the sea of life. The boat now enters into the eye of the storm. This is a place to rest, to reorganize, to take stock of the situation and the condition of the boat, and to get ready to enter the storm once again.

You can give yourself the calm of the eye of the storm by choosing to do so. You can take the time to take stock of the situation and create a plan of action to weather the 'storms' of life. Or, at the very least, get some greatly needed rest.

CHAPTER 2

Why do I want to take a SOLO?

Because you deserve it!

And, without it, you will never be all you can be.

"Each man has a choice in life. He may approach it as a creator or a critic, a lover or a hater, a giver or a taker."

Unknown

"Each of us goes through life reflecting on the experience and making conscience choices. Or, we drift on the wind currents that others create."

Carolyn Harvill

Each of us is special. There is no one else exactly like you. There will never be another you. We get so wrapped up in **living** that we don't take advantage of the opportunities to explore who we are.

In the *Artist's Way* Julia Cameron states, "When I treat myself as a precious object, I am strong." What does that mean? I believe it means when you value yourself, get to know who you are, and honor your life, you develop strength. You are then able to do the things that need to be done, as well as the things you were meant to do. You become congruent with who you are.

Have you ever felt disconnected from yourself? You see this person who is fulfilling the expectations of others as a spouse, a child, a parent, an employee, etc. These are also the expectations you put on yourself. Yet, you wonder who that person really is. Maybe you feel like you are running on autopilot. *Solos* can help you get in touch with who you really are and bring you to the point that <u>you</u> know <u>you</u> are piloting the plane.

As a mother of young children, I based many of my parenting decisions on the advice of others rather than what

I felt. My son and I spent years fighting over what he should eat. The only thing I accomplished was to create tension every time we shared a meal. But some people stared and made *comments* when they observed my son regularly eating peanut butter or hot dogs. This reinforced my feelings of being a *bad* parent. Hot dogs for breakfast really created comments. Therefore, we fought. I remember the precise moment when my son was eight that I decided that we were no longer going to fight over food. And, we didn't. He has always been very healthy and his friends and their mothers have expanded his food choices. Yes, he listened to others and not to me. Ah, one of the pleasures of parenting.

Becoming a stronger person benefits you and those around you. As you become congruent, you allow others to explore and express who they truly are.

When I made the decision to end my marriage of seventeen years, I was the only one who seemed to believe or understand that this truly was best for all concerned. I had a couple of friends who understood, but none in my family did. Over a decade later, my children now adults, who look back on what our lives were like before the divorce and what they are like now, we agree that it was a good thing for all of us.

From the moment the divorce was final, we no longer lived with the same friction, criticism, *teasing*, and stress that we endured before. I finally made decisions based on what was best for me, and supported my children in their decisions. Certainly life did not become easy or continue without stress, but it did contain more options and opportunities.

Solos were the fuel to understanding the situation. By stepping out of the storm and into the peace the 'eye of the storm' provided, I was able to see the whole situation and experience the courage to take the needed steps.

Here are six benefits of creating *Solos* in your life. I am sure that you will identify more as you enjoy your journey to self-discovery and self-validation.

1. Freedom - *Solos* can give you experiences of freedom. During your time away, whether 10 minutes or 10 days, you are in control of your time. You decide what to do and what to think about. It is *your* time.

Freedom can be scary. If you are making the decisions, you have no one to blame for the outcomes but yourself. We live in a time and place that loves to blame others for what happens to us. It has probably always been that way. A fast-food restaurant makes its coffee hot, only to get sued when a lady pours it on herself. The rains come and everyone says to Noah, "It's your fault we're wet, you should have warned us more often and used a louder voice!"

Freedom brings with it accountability and responsibility. If you are happy or unhappy, where you want to be or where you do not want to be, it is to yourself that you must look to find answers or to take actions that can change your situation. The awareness grows that you are the person responsible for where you are and that you have the power to make choices to change the situation. The power to make a new choice is yours.

Don't worry. The more *Solos* you take the more you will trust yourself, enjoy your freedom, and feel good about the control you are exercising. With trust of yourself, comes the willingness to take responsibility for your own situation.

This is the cure for feeling out of control and at the mercy of others and circumstances.

2. Time to reflect on your life. - Aristotle said, "A life unexamined is a life not worth living." It can be a life lived on autopilot that at the end is filled with regrets. Few regret what they have done; they regret what they failed to do. *Solos* give us the opportunity to examine our lives, set priorities, and discover our dreams. People who work with those that are dying say they hear the same two questions over and over again in different formats. Was I loved? Did I love well? Solos give us the opportunity to ask these questions throughout our lives and avoid regrets at the end of life.

3. It's fun! - Whether it is a walk, a movie, week of sightseeing, or two days by a river, it can be great fun. You define what fun is.

4. It's creative! - You could write a book, a song, a poem, knit an heirloom, or begin your autobiography. The opportunities are as varied as we are.

5. Appreciation - *Solos* build appreciation for yourself, the people in your life and the circumstances of your life. Or they will show which people and circumstances need changing in your life and provide the courage and energy to make those changes. Where is your life not working for you? Where is the pain in your life? Oprah Winfrey recommends a gratitude journal. Taking notice of the things that you appreciate will change your perspective and your life.

It is often easier to focus on the things we don't like and make ourselves miserable. When we pay attention to the things we do like our smiles come more quickly.

6. Perspectives - *Solos* offer perspective. You can step back and really see what is happening all around you. Is the situation you were so concerned about yesterday still on your list? If it is, maybe it is time to take action. Can you

remember why you were upset a week ago, last year? Can you remember why you were mad at a certain person last month? Without taking time to see things from a more remote view, we get mired in the mud of details and the rush of emotions.

All in all, you deserve the time to know and enjoy who you are! You not only deserve, but also desperately need to rest and strengthen your understanding of yourself and your situations. These things will allow you to chart the course of your deepest desires, to reach your greatest purpose. This is a true place of belonging and peace.

CHAPTER 3

When should I take a SOLO?

As often as possible!

Carolyn Harvill

"If you are lucky and reverent, and hush for a moment the voices of doubt in your head, sometimes God will whisper in your ear."

Kate Santich in Florida Magazine

A *Solo* can be as short as a few minutes or as long as a few weeks. *Solos* can be built into any schedule.

Starting with small amounts of time is important. Deciding to go off for a week by yourself when you are not used to spending time alone can be traumatic. Watching T.V. by yourself is not spending quality time with yourself, unless you are then reflecting on what you just watched. Remember, you are making a commitment to get to know yourself and listen to your heart. Give yourself time to get used to your own company.

How do you start learning to enjoy *Solos*? A great start is to begin with a few minutes once a week, and, as soon as you are comfortable, move to a few minutes each day. Remember, you are creating your special time. So, listen to your heart about how to begin and how quickly to extend your time. There will be many things to distract you. Recognize that. Don't worry about it. Stick to your commitment to yourself.

One suggestion - for each of the next four weekends, carve out thirty minutes to one hour for yourself. This could mean getting up early one morning before the house is awake. You might go shopping alone for one hour to find that journal, browse through a bookstore for a book that speaks to you, go to a park, enjoy your own backyard, or take a walk.

If you have not had the experience of wandering around a bookstore until a book calls your name, try it. Just walk around and read titles and look at the pretty covers until one just feels right. This is the one that is right for you right now.

You can easily spend an hour wandering around a bookstore. On the way home, think about how it feels to have an hour that is your own. If money is tight, go to the library.

Now begin to build a few minutes of *Solo* time into your days. Maybe you will begin with three days a week or everyday. This is unique to you and your schedule. There is no one right way.

From this small beginning, you will start to enjoy *Solos* at your own rate of speed and duration.

Remember not to 'should' all over your new commitment. If you plan three days and get one, celebrate the one! It will be easier to add the other two next week if you are celebrating the one this week.

Again, there is no one right time, place, or way to take a *Solo*. You are making a commitment to live a congruent life and to get to know the uniqueness of you. Many find early morning a good time. Others do not like the mornings. Find the time that is right for you. When you need to pick a new time, make the switch without guilt. We change and so do our schedules and preferences.

When my children were small, I heard the morning was the perfect time for solitude. I was told to just set my alarm clock a little earlier. I tried. I <u>really</u> tried. But, when I got all settled and ready to read, write, or think, all I wanted to do was sleep. It was not a productive time for me. My failure filled me with guilt. Finally one day I wrote in my journal, "Help! This is not working. I need more energy or a different plan." Then I dozed off.

Later that day the children were taking their naps. I had a great idea. (I can't imagine where the idea came from.) I would do my quiet time now and skip the soap opera. It worked. The fact that I was willing to skip my soap opera was surprising. But, it just felt right.

In the years that followed, I began to take multi-day retreats with a friend of mine. With all the naps we were taking, we decided that you could meditate when you sleep. We called it "napping in the Spirit." We would read a little or journal a little and then fall asleep. I think it was a case of being given what we needed most – rest.

Trust that you will be able to hear *you* speak. Sounds a little freaky, doesn't it? It isn't really. You have had hunches, feelings, insights, and just-knowing-that-you-know-what-to-do kinds of experiences. Those were you speaking to you, or as some would say, God speaking to you through you. However you think of this voice, listen to it. This same voice will guide you in making decisions about how, where, and when to take time for yourself.

CHAPTER 4

What do I do about resistance from others?

Stand firm.

"Yesterday I dared to struggle. Today I dare to win."

Bernadette Devlin

Unless you live alone and don't have relatives or friends involved in your life, or unless you can keep what you are doing a secret, you will face resistance.

I'm not sure why that is. Others fear growth in us for lots of reasons. However, that is a long psychological discussion for another book. I will say that if you can understand that resistance to change in others is just human nature and not vindictiveness directed at you, you will deal with it better and not let it hang you up or negatively influence your relationships.

You are doing something for you. Keep your commitment. Know that taking care of you is a worthwhile thing. Listen to your heart. Sometimes people, especially women, get caught in the *I have to make everyone else happy* trap. Oprah calls it the 'disease to please.' If you are there, remind yourself that when you take care of yourself, you have more to give to others.

When someone in your life voices objections, deal with the ones that are valid and ignore the invalid objections.

Valid - Often, there are real logistical issues that you will need to deal with.

"Who will baby-sit while you are away all morning?" "What will it cost?" You might be able to trade with a spouse or a neighbor for time away. Have a plan before the objection is voiced.

Invalid - This sort of objection needs to be responded to with one response that is repeated if necessary. You do not want to fall into the trap of defending yourself or justifying your actions. Either the person cannot, or chooses not to understand your need for time alone. All the words in the world without action, will not change the situation. Look at these possible objections:

"If you want to be away from me it means you don't love me."

Possible response – "You know how I feel about you. Time apart does not diminish those feelings. A good relationship is based on commitment and trust."

(You might put some energy into spending time with this person later. Knowing that all relationships need attention and focus.)

"You are a bad parent because you want time away from your children."

Possible response –"I'm sorry you feel that way. I know I am a good parent and this taking care of myself will make me a better one. I want my children to learn to trust themselves and live examined lives. For that reason, I need to live my life as a good example of learning and growing. "

This type of resistance can be very hard to deal with because it is emotion based. Think about how you want to respond and stick to it. If you allow emotions (guilt, for instance) to take over, you will fall into the trap of doing what others want you to do and ignoring your own wants and needs.

There is a time to think about the needs of the people in your life and how you might be a part of supporting those needs and providing encouragement. Notice the phrase "part of." None of us is responsible for the emotions of another. But, as a spouse, or a parent, we have committed to supporting another person the best way we can.

CHAPTER 5

What do I do about resistance from myself?

Acknowledge and keep moving.

Be not afraid of going slowly; be only afraid of standing still.

Chinese Proverb

"There isn't a person anywhere who isn't capable of doing more than they think they can."

Henry Ford

Most of us believe that to do something for ourselves is selfish. What is a *sel* fish anyway? Is it any kin to a clam?

Is it selfish for a corn plant to pull nutrients from the earth? Is it selfish for a cat to eat its cat food? No, it is survival. Feeding these systems what they need to survive and grow is necessary.

As human beings we need nourishment to be the best we can be and to offer nourishment to others. Alone times, *Solos*, are critical nourishment for our personal growth and survival. Oh, we could stay on autopilot all our lives. Or, we can consciously decide to take control of our own flight plans.

When the critical voice inside speaks up (we each have one), thank it for caring for you. Thank it for trying to protect you and then explain that this is important and move on. That little voice was necessary when you were a child. Your parents and all of society helped form it to protect you and *keep you in line*. Now it is time to get in touch with the real you. It is time to make decisions required to protect you. It is time to lead the life of your true choice and dare I say it – your true calling/your own uniqueness/ your giftedness.

When I was a little girl I often heard, "Don't talk so loud, little girls should have soft, gentle voices." When I began to speak professionally I heard, "Speak up! We can't hear you past the third row." In corporate meeting settings, I found that no one paid attention to my soft, gentle voice. It was time to rethink my soft voice. I decided that speaking with more enthusiasm and volume was a good thing.

I also grew up thinking that a husband and children were the *suppliers* of a woman's happiness. When I got my family, I would automatically be happy. Surprise! It didn't work that way. As the saying goes, I found out that **happiness is an inside job**. Don't worry, there is a real you and it is someone who will encourage you and support you and guide you into a more fulfilled and happy life. It may take a while to hear this voice over the shouts of the other critical voices. Honor your essence, and the voice of support and encouragement will get louder.

It's been said, "it is not one critical voice but a full committee." Our parents always leave us with voices in our heads. Moms seem to be champions at this. One of their greatest tools is guilt. But we also have teachers, siblings, friends, bosses, spouses, and even our children who can get in on the act. But our greatest critic is our own voice. Even changing a small percentage of our negative self-talk will change our lives. Getting our critic cheering instead criticizing for just a few minutes a day will be the fuel to move us towards our authentic self.

The largest block to great achievements is not the size of the challenge, but the self-doubt we hold in our hearts.

We also doubt that our gift is worthwhile. If we are not going to cure cancer, or be President of the United States, or be a famous rock star, then why bother? We forget that our gifts are unique. We may be the only who has a particular gift.

Freddie Hoffman started life with what many would say was a handicap. He had brain damage. Freddie has not lived the life that we think of as normal. He has not enjoyed the many things that most of us think of as valuable. He has never dated or driven a car. He has not been scholastically successful, had a lot of friends, or even read a great book. . His job is being a janitor in a church.

He was four before he took his first step. But, at age five, Freddie was given a tricycle, and a passion was born. While riding he felt normal and at peace. So, he kept riding. The most he has ridden in one day is 287 miles. A hundred miles a day is fairly normal... for Freddie. He started logging his miles at age seven. And at the age of 42, he has ridden in excess of 1.3 million miles. When his mother died of leukemia in 1986, he began to do fundraising for cancer research in her honor. In 2002, he had raised over $550,000. He is still ridding and raising funds.

Would any of us envy his gift? Probably not. Do we see the gifts that he gives to himself and to the world? When he is riding he is happy. He is a great example of finding what makes your heart sing and sticking with it. If that were as far as it went, that would still be a wonder. But, he has found a way to bless the world by raising funds for a worthwhile cause and to give so many others the opportunity to share in the joy of that endeavor.

Don't decide what are worthwhile gifts. Commit to finding your gift and giving it completely. So many people have said to me, "You tell me what my passion/gift is and I will live it to the fullest." A common frustration is that so often we just don't know. That's OK too. Actively search and be open to the surprises along the way. If you are like most of us, you will be surprised at what you find and what you share with the world. And for most of us it doesn't happen nearly as quickly as we would like for it to. The process is necessary. Trust it.

CHAPTER 6

What is a SOLO like?

What are you like?

"There is only one success - - to be able to spend your life in your own way."

Christopher Morley

There are as many ways to experience a *Solo* as there are people. You will find suggestions, guidelines and even *experts* who will tell you *exactly* how it is done. Use what is useful from these sources and then let you be you. This is about finding the uniqueness within. This will be expressed uniquely. 'Duh.'

No two are alike, even *Solos* for the same person. There are so many variables: the person; the amount of resistance; the emotional, spiritual, and physical state of the person; the materials read; the place; etc. You will always find opportunities for reflection, fun, and growth.

Truly being where you have a block of time to call your own creates the challenge of freedom. You learn a lot about yourself through your choices. THERE ARE NO WRONG CHOICES! This is not about following rules or being a certain way. It is about letting you be you!

When I first began in earnest to listen, what I really wanted was a skywriter. You know, the airplane with the message trailing behind. I would just look up to the sky and read what I was supposed to do, and how to do it, and life would be so simple. Reality set in. I needed to go inside and discover my path. My path would be one of discovery and unexpected twists and turns. And, oh such joy!

On the idea page, you will find several books that give specific ideas on how to structure a *Solo*. These are books that have been helpful to my friends or me. They may or may not be helpful to you. Bookstores are full of all sorts of books on retreats, meditation, etc. The right idea will come to you at the right time. Trust yourself to recognize what you need today and at every moment.

I have found that my experiences change over time. What worked for me last year or last month doesn't necessarily work now. That's OK. This is a process, not a destination.

When my children were small, taking *Solos* in the afternoons worked for me. Later, working in "Corporate America" was not conducive to using afternoons. I found that while morning *Solos* had not worked years ago, now they did. While I used to struggle to fill one page of my journal a day, after reading *The Artist's Way*, three pages a day is my norm. Will this change in the future? Probably.

If what you are doing is a struggle, you are probably listening to your mind or to someone else, but not to your heart. Spirituality/connectedness is your nature. It is who you are. Getting in touch with you takes time and commitment, but not struggle or pain. During your healing process you may experience pain, but the process of being with yourself does not require discomfort. If you are experiencing conflict you are probably judging the experience.

I'm not sure who first said it, but it is true: TRUST THE PROCESS. It may not go the speed or direction you would lay out but the process will move you closer to your hopes and dreams and knowing who you are.

The following is a list of *Solo* possibilities. See if any of these strikes a cord of recognition or desire in you.

• Five minutes in bed before you get up, think about the things that make you happy, or proud, or peaceful, or excited, or … .

• A walk in the park.

• Sitting in a rocking chair looking out on ____ .

• Watching a movie you want to see all by yourself. Go to the theater or watch at home late at night.

- Concentrate on the flickering of a candle. (This and other meditations clear the mind of clutter.)
- 'Napping in the Spirit.'
- Journaling.
- Reading.
- Writing.
- Crocheting.
- Bike riding.
- Massage.
- Facial.
- Music.
- Gardening.
- Conscious breathing.

When I first began to take *Solos*, I was putting on earphones and listening to music. My husband and children would be watching TV. Was I also trying <u>not</u> to listen to the TV? Yes. If I left the room, I would be a 'bad' parent and spouse.

I knew I needed time for me and this was the only way I could seem to get it. The demands of being a parent and a spouse were making me feel like I was drowning. I'm not sure how else to put it. Other than as a spouse, daughter, parent, or volunteer, I felt that I had no identity. Before this time I hadn't thought I needed one. I had accomplished my goals: got married and had children. Now what? Why wasn't I happy? Why didn't I feel fulfilled or at least content?

In the years since, I have found out a lot about myself. Some things I am very proud of. Others, I'm not so proud of, but I understand and accept them better. I now know that I really do care about other people. I am also highly critical of others. I discovered that it is OK to be in a quiet place. I used to be one of those people who immediately turned on the TV when they walk into a house. Now it comes on only if I am going to sit down and watch it. I value and enjoy a quiet home.

I truly value comfort; Not just as a convenience, but as a right and a requirement in my life. When I discovered this, I also needed to realize that it was OK to ask for what I needed. My comfort is a need. I had to accept that it did not make me a bad person (a sel-fish) to want to be comfortable. I know that I want good food, cool air, a soft bed, and comfortable clothes. And, that is OK.

I also learned that I can actively make choices to develop and express the characteristics and talents I choose. Learning to understand, and to acknowledge that you have choices and that you are making choices constantly is life changing. You go from victim to creator.

After a short time, I sporadically began to get up a little earlier for reading or my first attempts at journaling. Not a stellar start, but a start. Our hearts cry to be heard. Whatever response we give is celebrated.

My quiet times, my *Solos*, have helped me through many difficult times including going back to work from being a stay-at-home mom, divorce, empty nest, changing careers, losing loved ones, writing a book, and a multitude of other things. Sometimes I have been as regular as sunrise in my commitment. Other times I have been as scarce as raindrops during a Texas drought. The lessons learned have been varied, surprising, and repetitive. It seems some things are hard for me to hear, to change or to just accept.

Two of my toughest lessons have been: First, not wearing a size 12 does not make me a bad person. I am still a valuable person with things to share. Many of us define our worth by how we look and what we eat. This has been a thirty-year struggle for me. Second, there are actions taken by others that are not acceptable to me. It doesn't make them bad people. It just means I need to protect myself from their actions. And, I have a right to do so.

One very important lesson I want to try to share with you up front. I don't want it to take you as long to learn this one as it did me. ALL EFFORTS ARE BENEFICIAL. You CAN'T get it WRONG. TAKING TIME OFF HAPPENS. BE GENTLE WITH YOURSELF. Adjustments to your plans happen. OK, SOME DAYS TOTAL CHAOS HAPPENS. Commitments change. Maybe that's more than one lesson.

If you understand the previous paragraph, and are gentle with your starts and stops, you will move faster than you can imagine in ways that bring you joy. And if you don't - keep trying. Keep treating yourself as the precious one that you are.

What we honor prospers.

CHAPTER 7

What are the pitfalls to watch out for?

Shoulding all over yourself.

"You came into the world an original. Don't go out a copy."

Anonymous

It is such a temptation to judge ourselves. I <u>should</u> be more consistent. I <u>should</u> feel something different. I <u>should</u> journal three pages today. I <u>should</u> have made more progress. I <u>should</u> be able to concentrate more, etc., etc., etc. Pick your favorite should.

The direct result of *shoulding* is guilt. Guilt is a useless/debilitating/destructive emotion. (Regret is different.) Guilt and worry are like rocking chairs, they give you something to do, but they don't get you anywhere. Guilt not only doesn't get you anywhere but it robs you of the enjoyment of where you are. The fastest way to stop giving yourself time for yourself is to feel guilty about the time you miss, or the time you couldn't relax or concentrate. We all have times we feel really good about and times we don't feel so good about. So what! Enjoy the good ones and be gentle with yourself over the ones that were not so good.

Don't judge the experience. Who is to know what was a good day and what was not such a good day? The day that nothing seemed to happen may later show as an important day in your experience. It is <u>never</u> a waste to honor your commitments to yourself. When you keep your commitments, you are honoring and respecting who you are.

There have been many times when I wanted to get closure around an issue, or make a decision during a quiet time, and could not think or settle down. Within a day or two, more information would come to me that would completely change the situation. I was trying to rush a decision. Down deep, I knew I needed to wait. So times of indecision or confusion are not scary anymore. I just think, 'Well I must need more information. Or, the time is just not right.'

Through your commitment to honor yourself, you are getting to know who you are beneath the layers. Patience, any worthwhile relationship takes time. And this is truly the most worthwhile, life-long, relationship you will ever have.

A note about regret versus guilt: a lot has been written about the differences. Guilt has a way of eating away at you about something you cannot change. It has an element of giving up. Of thinking, "What is the use?" "I am a bad person." It keeps you from making good choices in the now. When you are feeling guilt, it is a time to ask yourself, "Is this a beneficial action or thought pattern for me to have? Is it moving me to good action or keeping me stuck in bad feelings?" Guilt is a thief of inner peace and self regard. It carries the message, "I am a bad person."

Regret is knowing that if you had it to do over again, you would do it differently. It may also be that you wish you could have learned that lesson in a less painful way. Regret is deciding that if that situation occurs again, you will deal with it in a different way. Regret also includes action either to correct or change something done or action to change future behavior. The message is, "I am a good person who made a bad choice".

CHAPTER 8

If I take a SOLO vacation will I ever be

able to vacation with others again?

Yes. If you choose to, you will.

"We are born and we die. Everything in between is negotiable."

"You are never given a desire without also being given the power to express it to the world. Live the opportunities, strive for your dreams, believe in yourself and you will create a life that brings you joy."

Carolyn Harvill

This chapter is the result of my first weeklong *Solo* vacation. I took the opportunity to go to New Mexico by myself. My journal and I went off on an adventure. It was the most freedom I had yet experienced. For a full week, all decisions were mine. All results were mine as well. After I got there, I had no responsibilities other than deciding where and when to eat dinner, etc.

Before I left, I had lots of advice from friends and family about what to see, what to do, and where to go. I took some of the advice and ignored the rest. I even ignored some of my own plans. I was so sure I would do certain things, and enjoy seeing certain places. I had a plan! It was somewhat of an effort to throw the plans out the window and just do what *I* wanted to do during each particular moment. Some of the changes were spending only hours instead of days in Santa Fe, and taking my first, and so far my only, hot air balloon ride.

The trip was a result of many years of short *Solos* that taught me it was a good thing to spend time alone and I deserved it. When I told people about my plans, they would make comments about how crazy they sounded. That much time alone would drive them nuts. My thoughts were, "Then maybe you should start with a few minutes a day to find out what a wonderful and fun-to-be-with person you are?"

The first night, as I sat alone in the Best Western, I thought, "Are you crazy, this was a terrible idea!" The flight was OK. Getting the rental car was a nightmare. Finding the motel took several U-turns to correct my destination detours. It was 9:00 PM. I was alone watching lousy TV in a motel room by myself eating snacks from the vending machine. I felt alone and concerned about the money I was spending on this **crazy** trip. How could I justify spending money to travel to a place to watch TV?

By the next day at noon, I had settled in and given myself permission to just be and enjoy. If I wanted to watch lousy TV, then OK. In reality, I only watched TV one other night and that was to watch one of my favorite shows. I did not have to justify what I wanted to do to anyone, including myself.

The freedom of a week where you can do or be anything, can take some getting use to. If you have never eaten in a restaurant alone, you need to try it. Have you ever bought just one ticket to a museum or a movie or amusement park? You get some strange stares. But, when the people notice the contented smile on your face, their stares may turn to looks of envy or admiration.

About half way through the week, I thought this was the absolute best vacation I had ever had. And, it was.

Maybe because I am a mother, most vacations before, were spent trying to keep peace between Dad and the children, between the children, or between my friends. It seemed that no matter who was on the trip, we could never all agree on what we wanted to do and the speed with which we wanted to do it. Just deciding on a restaurant was a challenge. This is not true when you travel alone. I could eat anyplace I wanted and stay by the river as long as I wanted. OOOOh it was bliss.

That's when I began to think that; I would never travel with anyone else again.

But I have and I will continue to enjoy travel with others.

While *Solos* are wonderful, they are different experiences from shared vacations. There is a place for both. Each offers enjoyment.

In the same year I took a Solo to New Mexico, I went to Seattle and the Northwest with my daughter. It was the first time my adult daughter and I had taken a trip with just the two of us. Wow! A few years into adulthood and she is more than the wonderful person she has always been, she is the perfect travel companion. We found out that we like to see the same types of things and we sightsee at the same speed. It was a wonderful time of sharing the enthusiasm and the enjoyment of discovery.

So it is not only *Solo* vacations or shared vacations, it is the richness of both types of experiences.

CHAPTER 9

Will it hurt?

Probably.

Carolyn Harvill

"What we call results are beginnings."

Ralph Waldo Emerson

When we take time to look at our lives, we open doors to appreciating who we are and how we live. We also open the possibility of seeing things that need changing, things with which we are not happy, or things that cause friction instead of peace.

When we start to see things that need changing, it is because we are getting strong enough to make those changes. We may not want to change. We may not trust our own strength. But, when we see the need for change, we have the knowledge and tools and strength we need to make the changes. Sometimes what is lacking is the willingness. That is when our prayer might be; *I am willing to be willing.*

I mentioned that my first *Solos* included sitting in a chair listening to music or sometimes it was reading a book while the house buzzed around me. From that point it took years to fully accept why I felt so much pain. On the surface my life was good; husband, children, stay at home mom, and a volunteer at school and church. If life was so good, why did I feel so bad?

It was a three year process from the time we first began to say openly, "Something isn't working," before my husband and I decided that not only were we not helping each other, we were doing damage. I wonder how people go through so much pain without the comfort of a journal. It gave me a place to vent my anger where I wouldn't hurt anyone else. Instead of saying angry words to the people around me, I put them in my journal and let them go. It gave me a place to clarify what was happening and how I was feeling. For me, it was a thread to hold onto.

During that time, I also had the opportunity to meet with a psychologist. Having someone to talk to so openly changed my life.

Looking back if personal coaches had been available, that is the way I would have gone. I needed someone who would listen, and when appropriate, plant seeds for making changes.

Life is change. No matter how much we would like for it to stay the same, life by its very nature is change. If things are not changing you are either dead or growing barnacles. Remember, the only person who will go through all of that change with you is you. You are an important person to get to know and trust.

While life is change, we often just let it happen to us. This knowing ourselves will call us to make changes, not just let them happen. This can look too painful. Remember to trust the process. The initial stages can be painful, but the results will be more congruency and joy.

CHAPTER 10

Tell me one more time - Why take

SOLOS?

You need them.

"Freedom from guilt? Yes, put your energy where it can make a difference vs. being self-absorbed in guilt about past events."

"Motivation – the anticipation of achievement. We are what we have been becoming. Where are your focus, your thoughts, and your energies placed today? That is where <u>you</u> will be tomorrow."

Carolyn Harvill

The only way to *know* a person is to spend time with that person. This is especially true when you want to know yourself.

Most of our waking days and hours are spent with other people. We are reacting to other people and circumstances. We learn some things about ourselves during those times. But, is that all there is to know? And is that really who we are or just how we have learned to react to others?

Have you ever had friends you thought you knew? Then one day, because of a word they said, or something they did, or a question they asked, you knew them in a whole new way. You thought you knew them before. You had been friends for a long time. But, all of a sudden, you knew them at a deeper level. You had a new perspective of who they were, or what they were capable of.

I found out that a friend had once been a member of the Polar Club. Members of the Polar Club take a dip in a frozen lake on the coldest day of the year. Why? I have no idea! I had never thought of her as someone who would do something so strange, daring, or just plain crazy. My friend, who had been the epitome of conservative behavior, took on a totally new aspect in my eyes.

This is the kind of thing that can happen when you spend time alone with a friend, or *yourself.*

During a quiet time years ago, I was reading a book. With tears in my eyes and a major lump in my throat, I wrote in my journal, "I want to write a book that will help people know themselves better." I immediately thought, "Surrrre, Who would want to read a book by you?" My little critical voice had kicked in. It was years later in New Mexico that I thought, "It is time to write my first book." First book? Hey, I *have* come a long way.

Dreams, like writing a book, are born and become realities in quiet times.

Lighten up! Don't take *Solos* or yourself too seriously. Many bad things have happened when some people have taken themselves too seriously. No doubt, wars, persecutions, broken relationships, and depressions are results of people seeing things in black & white, absolutes of right & wrong, all or nothing.

Have fun! More good things happen when people are having fun than when they are *deadly* serious. That's certainly an interesting phrase. Being gentle with *you* requires laughter and joy. Don't forget to smile at yourself and with yourself. A smile costs nothing but its benefits are extensive. A smile enhances physical, emotional, and spiritual well-being.

There is so much being written about the physical and emotional effects of smiles and laughter. When you look in the mirror in the morning or in a plate glass window you are passing, smile. This simple habit will transform your days.

CHAPTER 11

How do I maximize my enjoyment and the benefits?

Journal.

"Write as if there are no limitations in tomorrow. Doing so, you create your tomorrows. From your pen to God's ears, <u>and</u> yours."

Carolyn Harvill

I told you I would get back to journaling. Whether you have never kept a journal before, or have been doing it for years, the act of writing down your thoughts and feelings is a powerful tool of self-discovery.

Journaling is an aid to self-reflection. It also is a record of your journey. When I came across my note from so many years ago about writing a book, it was a moving experience. I had forgotten that day, but the desire and joy all came flooding back. And somehow, the courage to begin came with them.

A journal is a memoir for you to enjoy for years to come whether it is detailing a particular day, or your dreams for the future. You can return to it for renewed memories, direction and encouragement. You can read it on your next *Solo* and see how far you have come, or how far you have yet to go. Remember, there are no rules for you to follow. Just follow your heart.

During a *Solo*, your journal helps to give focus and direction, or just keep a record of events. In the list of ideas, there are several books referenced that talk about the value and how-tos of journaling. These books can be very helpful.

If you don't have such a book, just start writing. Don't worry about grammar, spelling, run-on sentences, sentence fragments, or any of that. Suspend all criticism of content, *appropriate* words or ideas, and whether it all makes sense. Just write what comes to mind; the profound, the tedious, the mundane, and the profane. Just let it flow. And if it doesn't flow, write anyway for a predetermined amount of time or space. Some say three pages a day. Ehhhh, start with a page or ten minutes and see where it goes.

Possible idea starters -

- Activities in my day
- What I am feeling
- My childhood
- My dreams
- Who I am mad at
- Describing a rose outside my window
- What I liked about the movie I saw last night
- What I most like about me and why
- What makes me happy or sad
- Anything and everything *I* want to write about!

This is not a list to follow, just a few thoughts to get you started.

This is important. You need to know that no one will read your journal. If you can't tell the people in your household to stay out and trust them, get a lock or hide it and DO NOT tell them what you are doing.

You can use a small notebook and put it in your purse or pocket. The problem is that you acquire a lot of journals over a period of time. A notebook can fill up very quickly.

I can't think of getting rid of mine, they mean too much to me. They are my friends. My daughter has promised to burn them when I am gone without looking at them. I trust her. Besides, they would bore her silly. Or maybe, shock her.

I'm sure people have gone on the quest for self-discovery without writing down one thing and done just fine. But, memories fade and we need encouragement that we are moving. We need a friend that we can tell everything to without fear of disapproval. A journal can offer us these things and more.

I am also sure that those who journal have a powerful tool that will help them along life's way. It is also true that commitments written down have more power than those only whispered in the mind.

CHAPTER 12

Is this religious?

Maybe. Maybe not.

"God is not in man like a raisin in a roll, but like the ocean in a wave."

Eric Butterworth

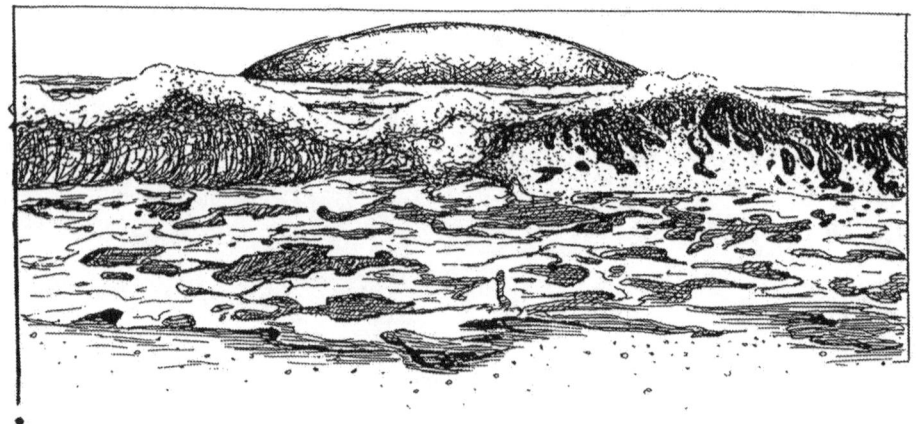

Many people who have embarked on a journey of self-discovery have found something that connects them with the universe, other people, and a higher purpose. There are many names, Great Spirit, the Universe, the Holy Spirit, Spirit, Jesus, Buddha, the Higher Self, God, the Great Unconscious, and countless more.

Setting aside time for yourself may lead you to one of these or strengthen your faith. So while *Solos* are not attached to one religion, they are certainly spiritual and at home in many religious practices.

All faiths talk about connection, being part of a whole, fulfilling a purpose. When you get past the *rules* and *traditions* of any religion to the connection part at the center, you are into spirituality.

A few highlights of my background include: being raised in the Baptist tradition, attending an Episcopal Church, graduating from a three year ecumenical spiritual direction program, teaching an Episcopal four year program that goes from Genesis to Revelations to the Reformation, writing this book from a Catholic retreat center, and loving several *New Age* writers.

What I have found in all of these experiences, are people trying to make sense of life. In every place and circumstance there are people who know that there is more to life than what we can see and touch. These are people who talk about something greater than any one individual and yet no more important than just one person. Many of these people talk about <u>strengthening their understanding and connection by spending time alone</u>.

I have never found anyone who regretted making such a commitment.

A commitment to simple spirituality, the practice of taking *Solos*, is a commitment to respect and honor the uniqueness of you. This commitment is the eye-of-the-storm to keep us from being 'whelmed.' Though it may seem we are overwhelmed. We never are. There is always that core within us that is waiting for discovery. This core wants to show us how to appreciate our value and know that the best is yet to come!

Exploring your essence will act as the wind to fly the hot air balloon that is your life ever higher and higher. This exploration through Solos will put you in sync with your essence and create the courage and determination to live your life to the fullest!

My hope for you is that ...

You will gift yourself with SOLOS often. Your Solos lengths will grow and their impacts in your life are felt more each year.

You will learn to know yourself more.

You will grow in appreciation for the gifted unique creation that you are.

Your choices will be more conscious choices. Your joy in life will be abundant.

Please, always be gentle with yourself. Remember to enjoy the simplicity. I trust that as you share this newfound appreciation for yourself and your connection to the whole, your talents will blossom and the world will be a better and more congruent place for all of us.

Carolyn

"Expect your every need to be met, expect the answer to every problem, expect abundance on every level, expect to grow spiritually. You are not living by human laws. Expect miracles and see them take place. Hold ever before you the thought of prosperity and abundance, and know that doing so sets in motion forces that will bring it into being."

Eileen Caddy, whose Findhorn Community on the northernmost coast of Scotland is internationally known for growing an abundance of plants, vegetables, fruits, and herbs in the worst conditions, is credited with the above quote.

The Idea Page

Many of these are my personal favorites. There are also personal favorites suggested by friends. I would love to hear of your favorites. These are just a few suggestions to get you started.

This list reflects a wide range of books and tapes. There is a story about a Priest who invited all sorts of people to present to his congregation because he knew they needed more teaching than he could offer. One night after a presentation by someone totally different from the congregation, a member was fussing and asking why the Priest had invited such a man to present. His answer, 'Keep the meat and throw away the bones.' Take what is of benefit to you and let the balance pass by.

You will notice that many of these books are in story form to share spiritual concepts. They make for easy reads with thought provoking ideas.

- <u>The Alchemist</u> by Pavlo Chelho
- <u>The Anatomy of the Spirit</u> tape series by Carolyn Myss. It started as a book, but I prefer the tapes.
- <u>The Artist's Way</u> by Julia Cameron
- <u>A Tree full of Angels</u> by Macrina Wiederkehr
- <u>The Holy Bible</u>
- Books by Neale Donald Walsh, my favorites are <u>Conversations with God One</u> and <u>Friendship with God</u>.
- Books by Og Mandino
- <u>Celebrate Yourself</u> by Eric Butterworth
- The <u>Chicken Soup for the Soul</u> books.
- <u>Count your Blessings</u> by Dr. John F. Demartini
- <u>Dance of Anger</u> by Harriet G. Lerner
- <u>Gift from the Sea</u> by Anne Morrow Lindbergh
- <u>God Calling</u> edited by A. J. Russell
- The <u>Harry Potter</u> Books by J. K. Rowling – Just plain fun.
- <u>The Invitation</u> by Oriah Mountain Dreamer
- <u>Kitchen Table Wisdom – Stories that Heal</u> by Rachel Naomi Remen, M. D.

- <u>Meditations: A Woman's Personal Journal, with Quotations.</u> Blank pages for you to fill in.

- Music offers something for every taste. Whether it is Gospel, Gregorian chant, Classical, Country, Jazz, or whatever, there is something for everyone and for all our different moods.

- <u>Please Understand Me</u> – The Myers-Briggs System

- <u>Psycho-Cybernetics</u> by Maxwell Maltz, M. D., F. I.C.S.

- <u>Seek my Face</u> by William A. Barry S.J.

- <u>Seven Habits of Highly Effective People</u> by Stephen R. Covey

- <u>The Simple Abundance Journal of Gratitude</u> by Sarah Ban Breathnach

- <u>St. George and the Dragon</u> by Edward Hays. His other books are great as well. They make you think in new ways and they are fun to read.

- <u>Wisdom of Florence Scovel Shinn</u> by Florence Scovel Shinn

- <u>Writing to Grow: Keeping a Personal-Professional Journal</u> by Mary Louise Holly

I love this article about Jim Carrey. We don't think of what it is that got an actor to the top. Most of the time we think of it as luck. Jim has a different theory.

Yes Man

For all his wild comedy, actor Jim Carrey is an introspective man. The star of *Liar, Liar* and *Ace Ventura: Pet Detective* took flight from his reign as the king of physical comedy with *The Truman Show,* and more recently, *Man on the Moon,* about the late comedian Andy Kaufman.

Although a high school dropout, Carrey is known to friends as someone who lives an examined life. He uses what he calls affirmations to bolster himself. Years ago, before a breakthrough in his career, he sat in a decaying car that he'd bought with leftover sitcom money and told himself, "I am one of the top five actors. Every director wants to work with me." Then he wrote himself a check inscribed, "For acting services rendered, $10 million."

Carrey attributes all the good things in his life to his affirmations, which he derives from self-help and spiritual literature. Now such thoughts come while he is in solitude. These days he'll slip quietly into his pool. "That's where I swim and float and talk to God and do whatever," says Carrey. "And a lot of good things have happened there."

Steven Daly in *Vanity Fair*

93

Carolyn Harvill

The next several pages are for your notes. They also pose a question or an idea for your reflection. This may be a way to start or enrich your journal.

I appreciate . . . .

I look forward to . . .

Carolyn Harvill

I hate it, but I have to . . . .

I like to think about . . .

I wish I could. . . .

I wish I could forget . . .

I am happiest when . . .

My philosophy of life is .

For additional copies or more information about Life Stories and Carolyn Harvill, please contact us at. **713-686-0798**

carolyn@carolynharvill.com

www.carolynharvill.com

About the Author:

Carolyn Harvill went from stay-at-home Mom to Purchasing Manager for The Minute Maid Company. These are two very different worlds that require totally different skills.

During her rise in corporate life, she went back to school for nine years to get her Bachelor's degree, completed a four year course in lay ministry, a three year course in spiritual direction, and finalized a divorce while raising two teenagers. She understands stress and the need to find an inner core of strength. This book is one of the ways that Carolyn shares what she has learned. Carolyn also presents programs of humor, motivation and inspiration for associations and businesses across America.

www.ingramcontent.com/pod-product-compliance
Lightning Source LLC
Chambersburg PA
CBHW020609300526
45785CB00021B/1404